The Kingfish

OTHER PLAYS

by Larry L. King

The Best Little Whorehouse in Texas
1977
The Night Hank Williams Died
1985
Christmas: 1933
1986
The Golden Shadows Old West Museum
1987

by Ben Z. Grant

From Hardscrabble
1990

Originally produced by
Barbara S. Blaine
at New Playwrights' Theatre,
Washington, D.C., 1979
First professional production
starred John Daniel Reaves
Larry L. King, Director
Larry L. King & Alix King, Set Design
Tomm Tomlinson, Lighting Design
Jackie English, Sound

Authors Ben Z. Grant and Larry L. King show the
many sides of Huey Long and reflect what they believe to
be his attitudes. They have invented dialogue when
illustrating historical events. They have brought Long
back from the grave to comment on current or recent
politicians and events. They have permitted
him to relive and discuss his own assassination.
The Kingfish *melds fact and fancy.*

The Kingfish

A one-man play loosely depicting the life and times of the late Huey P. Long of Louisiana

Larry L. King & Ben Z. Grant

Southern Methodist University Press

Dallas

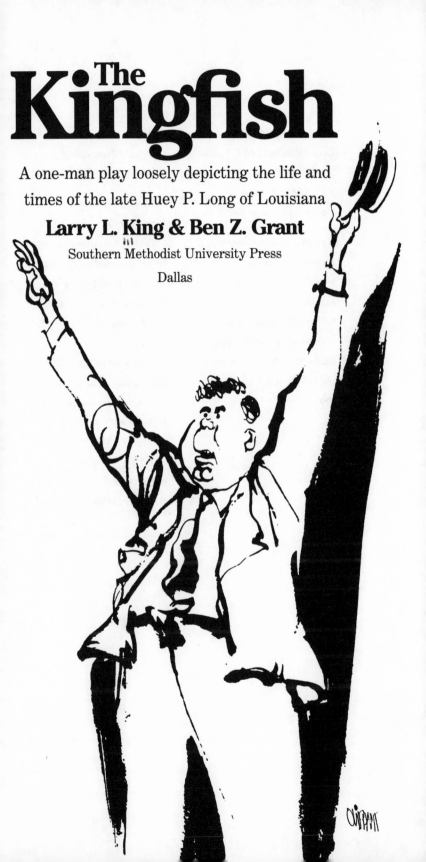

Cover and title page illustration by
Oliphant © June, 1979
Book design by Richard Hendel

Cataloging-in-Publication Data
King, Larry L.
    The kingfish : a one-man play
loosely depicting the life and times
of the late Huey P. Long of
Louisiana / by Larry L. King and
Ben Z. Grant.
    p. cm.
    ISBN 0-87074-324-4. – ISBN
0-87074-325-2 (pbk.)
    1. Long, Huey Pierce, 1893–
1935–Drama. I. Grant, Ben
Z., 1939–.
    II. Title.
PS3561.I48K56   1992   91-52778
812'.54–dc20 CIP

This book is for the

original producer of

The Kingfish:

BARBARA S. BLAINE

With special thanks to

John Daniel Reaves,

Ken Parnell,

Ev Lunning, Jr., and

John McConnell:

our stage "Kingfishes," all

PREFACE

I think of *The Kingfish* as the little play that refused to die.

It premiered with a 21-performance run at the 128-seat New Playwrights' Theatre in Washington, D. C. in the summer of 1979. Despite generally good notices and receptive audiences, I considered the play something of a failure because I viewed the material as worthy of a big musical comedy complete with dancing girls, trombones, flashy costumes, and glitzy sets. Flushed by the new success of *The Best Little Whorehouse in Texas*, I was eager for a Broadway encore.

Co-author Ben Z. Grant had a one-man show in mind from the beginning. The mono-drama format appealed to me only because it was affordable. We would be starting with what I thought of as a showcase production certain to reveal the work's marvelous musical comedy potential. Toward that end, we had our stage Huey P. Long interact with many invisible companions rather than confining him to the usual out-front monologue; we used appropriate recorded music by Randy Newman as well as recordings of the real-life theme song Long claimed to have written, *Every Man a King*. While loosely depicting the life and times of the bombastic, controversial Louisiana politician, we chose to highlight his comic aspects over his darker side.

As the show's producer, my wife-lawyer-agent, Barbara S. Blaine, provided the $10,000 necessary to mount the one-man version and did all the business and practical ditchdigging things a producer must do, while visibly pregnant with our daughter Lindsay. She had to constantly reject the *grandioso* schemes of the director –

yours truly – and the actor, John Daniel Reaves, to assure that we wouldn't bust her budget by about $15,000. Artists not understanding about money, and producers not understanding about artists, there were nights when the main course at our dinner table was simmering tension.

But Barbara Blaine's tough frugality permitted a final profit, even though tickets were sold at the fire-sale price of $5.00 each. Admittedly, the profit was modest: $14.68 above our $10,000 cost, to be precise. Barbara awarded the full sum to Ben Z. Grant, who'd had the original idea for the show and then had invited me aboard as his writing partner. That $14.68 check, framed, now hangs in the law chambers Ben Z. Grant occupies as a judge on the Texas Court of Appeals in Texarkana. When it was issued I was certain it represented the last cent *The Kingfish* ever would earn.

My bleak conviction stemmed from watching the Broadway biggies we lured to our one-man show: they seemed to view it with blind eyes in terms of its musical comedy charms. Some left the theater scudding away sideways, like so many crabs escaping the firepot, waving good-night from safe distances, calling of airplanes to be caught, commitments to keep. Mike Nichols and his producing partner, Lewis Allen, temporarily raised blood pressures by showing interest – but, in the puzzling tradition of show-biz, suddenly cut off communications as if our telephones had been disconnected. Stephanie Phillips, the Broadway producer of *Whorehouse*, advised us to retain the one-man show format and send it on a tour of college campuses. This advice was not appreciated by one who had stood in Broadway's bright spotlight and had heard Broadway's siren song. I soon muttered oaths as an angry epitaph for *The Kingfish* and abandoned it for dead.

But southerners who had seen the one-man show in Washington kept it fitfully alive through occasional one-night stands at conventions or other gatherings. John Daniel Reaves first performed it in that humbler circumstance for the Alabama Bar Association; somebody who saw it there invited him to Georgia. There were performances for the Louisiana State Society and the Louisiana Congressional delegation. Reaves also did the show at fund-raisers benefitting some politicians in Texas and in Washington in the early-to-mid 1980s.

No professional producers or theaters sought the work, however, until 1988 when two Louisiana showmen, Perry Martin and Ron Simeral, obtained the rights in order to showcase the talents of actor John McConnell. Their production played New Orleans and Baton Rouge and then went on to tour just about every hamlet in Louisiana, including Huey Long's hometown of Winnfield; there were along the way a few side excursions into East Texas. In early 1990 the Harrell Performing Arts Theatre, just outside Memphis, gave *The Kingfish* its "Mid-Atlantic Premiere," starring Ken Parnell. Live Oak Theatre in Austin performed the show in 1990 and again in 1991 with Ev Lunning, Jr., as the stage Huey Long. All this activity seemed quite amazing to me, considering that the play had not been published anywhere until now; those wanting to produce it had to obtain and decipher the smudged, decade-old manuscript that had issued from my ancient Smith-Corona.

When a Louisiana group led by producers Michel Claudet and Darryl K. Christen in mid-1990 raised $400,000 and announced plans to take *The Kingfish* and John McConnell to New York, I was frankly skeptical – if hopeful – as to its chances for success. An earlier group of potential investors had been dissuaded by a veteran general manager who had opined, "A one-man play about a dead southern politician would be risky business in New York." But the Louisiana group persisted, opening *The Kingfish* at the Off-Broadway John Houseman Theatre on March 24, 1991. Despite good-to-excellent reviews, it lasted but five weeks in the recession market and in a time when New York audiences have repeatedly proved that they won't in hordes shell out big bucks unless offered musical extravaganzas or Neil Simon comedies.

Still, by fits and starts, always breathing just enough to stay alive through a dozen years, *The Kingfish* has outlived the small Washington theater where it began . . . to say nothing of surviving my long-damped expectations. And even at this writing, the stubborn Louisiana producers are considering a tour of college campuses and select small professional theaters. The play's history persuades me we have not yet seen the last of *The Kingfish*.

As to the play itself, we have taken some artistic liberties. Many of the utterances and incidents depicted are true, yes, though we have tried merely to steer our vehicle between the historical fencerows rather than be fanatics about accuracy. We did, after all, bring Huey Pierce Long, Jr., back from the grave to comment on his assassination and contemporary politics; we permitted him to view the people and events of his time with that perfect hindsight resulting from a distance of almost a half-century; we endowed him with his real-life megalomania. All these techniques distort reality and discourage pure truth.

The undisputed facts about Huey Long are these: born in Louisiana in 1893, he became a successful country lawyer and political populist. At age twenty-five he was elected state railroad commissioner. In that office, and as a member of the Louisiana Public Service Commission, he warred on big corporations and fought with conservative newspapers and any group or individual critical of him. His constituency was the common man . . . woolhats . . . rednecks . . . the have-nots. Elected governor in 1928, at the age of thirty-five, Long built a personal political machine so powerful that when he became a United States senator he hand-picked his statehouse successor and continued to rule Louisiana as his own grand duchy; those who got in his way were steamrolled without regard for the niceties.

By the time he was assassinated in 1935 at age forty-two, Huey Long was considered by many to be a threat to unseat President Franklin D. Roosevelt; others considered him a threat to the democratic system. Huey Long attracted, and repelled, millions of people with his "Share-the-Wealth" movement and an aggressive, flamboyant personal style; he was at once loved and hated, revered and feared. I think it fair to say that if he built, he also destroyed.

The reactions of theatergoers and critics alike to *The Kingfish* tend to be tied to the ideological baggage they bring to the theater. Like the politician, like the play; dislike the politician, dislike the play. The most persistent criticism has been that we didn't get enough of Long's menace on stage, papering over his sins with self-serving humor. There might be a little truth to that charge: we have admitted to being more fascinated by Huey Long than repelled by him. Indeed, we may be favorably disposed toward politicians by nature and training – Ben Z. Grant has served as a member of the Texas legislature and I once worked as a Congressional staffer. Besides,

I've always rather liked colorful rascals, and I suspect the same may be true of Ben Z. Grant despite his current judicial trappings.

In retrospect, I think our stage Huey P. Long could hardly avoid getting the upper hand in *The Kingfish*. Here is a master politician, full of ego, talking of that subject dearest to all politicians – *himself!* So how could he *not* win the day? Here is a lawyer who rarely lost a case: how could he *not* persuasively argue his own? I, for one, have enjoyed seeing him do it.

Larry L. King

The Kingfish

SET DESIGN

Center stage, rear, is an elevated podium the actor will use when depicting Huey Long on the campaign trail. That part of the podium facing the audience shall sport a big campaign-type poster of the actor playing the Kingfish.

Behind and above the podium is a movie screen on which to project the opening still photos of life in Louisiana in the 1930s, more fully described in the text of this play.

Stage right, rear, is an executive desk flanked by U.S. and Louisiana flags. The desk holds a telephone, an ashtray, a couple of books, a legal paper containing the impeachment charges against the Kingfish, and assorted desk clutter. Behind the desk is an executive chair; two chairs for visitors are slightly downstage right from the desk.

Stage left, rear, is the facade of an old, unpainted country cabin with a small porch. It may contain a rocking chair for the Kingfish to sit in, or the rocking chair may be eliminated and the actor can sit on the edge of the porch itself.

Slightly downstage left from the cabin is the stump of a tree.

A footstool is positioned near the footlights, center stage. Sometimes the actor will sit on it, though at one point he will briefly stand on it in illustrating a story about a campaign speech he once made.

Spotlights should be provided for each of these stage areas; generally the stage will be dark except for the area where the actor is working in a given moment.

PROPS

Cigars

Skimmer straw hat

Book of matches

Pocket bandanna

Tin bucket labeled "Cottolene"

A newspaper on desk

Legal document of impeachment on desk

Telephone on desk

Two books on desk

Desk clutter

Reading glasses

SOUND EFFECTS

1   A tape of Randy Newman's song "Louisiana," to be played during the use of still photographs at the outset of the play. (Cautionary note: Legal arrangements for the use of this music shall be the responsibility of the producer of each production of this play, in accordance with the copyright provisions pertaining to such music; such permission cannot be granted by the authors of *The Kingfish*.)

2   Sounds of an audience cheering, repeated several times during the production.

3   Large group of people talking: rather like cocktail party jabber; no distinguishable words.

4   Shouting; people yelling "Point of order" and "This is an outrage"; griping, grumbling, angry discontent.

5   A waltz tune.

6   A single gunshot and a yell.

7   Rapid gunshots, ricochet effects, interspersed with shouts and scuffling and running footsteps.

8   Ambulance sirens.

9   The deathbed comments of the Kingfish himself.

10   Music of "Every Man a King," the Huey Long theme

song, to be used at the conclusion of the play as the actor takes his curtain call.

ACT ONE

The stage opens dark. We hear music, VOICE OVER; it is Randy Newman's "Louisiana." We see old still photographs of the rural America of the 1930s, projected on a large rear screen: farmers, mules, breadlines, ragged children, migrant workers, country crossroads stores, courthouses. These are interspersed with still photos of HUEY P. LONG *making speeches, shaking hands, and so on. Music continues throughout this slide show.*

HUEY P. LONG (VOICE OVER)

If events continue as they now are, and circumstances are what they appear to be, it's almost certain I will be a candidate for the office of president of the United States in nineteen thirty-six.

(Slide show continues for about twenty seconds.)

And the masses of America, 75 to 80 to 85 percent of the people, not only give up their property year after year but they go further and further . . .

(Music and slides fade; we see HUEY LONG *in person, as spotlight picks him up near center stage rear, talking in concert with the voice over recording.)*

. . . and further and further and further into economic slavery to where the flesh and blood of the born and the unborn will never be able to raise the debt, let alone come

7

back and rescue the properties they've lost from these depressions.

(Music and slides end; spotlight goes out on the actor.)

ANNOUNCER (VOICE OVER)

Ladies and gentlemen, put your hands together and let's hear it for the Kingfish himself – the Honorable Huey P. Long!

(Into a single spotlight – grinning and waving his hat – steps HUEY P. LONG. He is dressed in a double-breasted white plantation suit; his hat is a flat straw skimmer. Applause is heard VOICE OVER. HUEY basks in it. He beams, waves, nods, mouths: "Thank ya . . . Thank ya . . . God bless . . . Thanks a bunch." Obviously, he is doing nothing to stop the ovation. As it dies, he cocks his head to the right and grins.)

THE KINGFISH

Now ain't that sweet music?

Except for the sound of money rattlin', or maybe good meat sizzlin' in the pan, I can't think of a *thing* that can hold a candle to the sound of two or more hands clappin'. And once a politician has heard such music, you know, it's mighty hard thereafter to settle for mere violins.

(He puts his hat on his head.)

My old daddy took me to a political pie supper down in

Louisiana when I was a little nubbin' – no more'n eight, nine years old – and it was a thing of wonder to me that a man could get up and brag on himself, be cheered for it, and maybe even get *paid* for it.

From that moment on, I was spoiled for honest work.

(He takes a cigar from his coat pocket and begins to unwrap it. He will use this cigar, and others, like a baton: waving it, poking it at the audience, using it for emphasis. Only rarely does he light it, and then he takes only perfunctory puffs.)

Well, it's mighty good to be back. Sure is.

I've been gone, ya know, since 19-and-35. *(A beat.)* If you don't mind me sayin' so, y'all have sure let this old world go to hell in a handbasket during my absence.

There wadn't any jet planes when I was here, or any television – lucky for my opponents! It was puredee hard-scrabble back then. A poor tough bugger playin' in the National Football League didn't make much more money than a one-armed cotton picker. Money wadn't much more than a memory to most folks.

I've heard it said that mine was a simpler time. Probably it was. I know it was a *hungrier* time. I was on the verge of changin' all that with my Share-the-Wealth program. Until a damn fellow shot me.

(He looks into the distance, pensive and still.)

9

Never did understand exactly why. I doubt if *he* knew why he did it. Hell, the man was a goddamned *stranger* to me! I always thought it was ironic – me havin' so many personal enemies who'd have dearly loved to kill me – that a stranger got there first.

(He fidgets his way to the stage apron at center stage;
it's as if he's trying to get closer to the audience,
to really take it into his confidence.)

I'd just come down from the top floor of the state capitol there in Baton Rouge, see. Even though I was a United States senator by then – no longer the governor – I still spent worlds of time in Louisiana. Louisiana was my power base, the well from which the water flowed. And a smart man will keep his eyes on his well to make sure nobody poisons it.

I ran the state through my hand-picked successor as governor – one O. K. Allen. Some people claimed he got his name from saying "okay" to everything I told him to do. They told it on O. K. Allen that he signed so many papers I shoved in front of him that one day a *leaf* blew in the window and he signed it before I could stop him.

O. K. might not of been any Quiz Kid, but he was my kinda man. Why, I could of picked his pocket and told him I was just lookin' for a match.

(He grins, produces a pack of matches
and lights his cigar.)

Some thought it was fittin' and proper that I got shot in

the corridor of the monument they say I'd built to myself. And it *was* the finest state capitol in America. Ya see, I understood about symbolism. Hell yes: you don't have to be a Yankee professor to understand a little somethin' about human nature.

The poor folks at the bottom of the pile – the rednecks, the woolhats, the have-nots – they needed a little somethin' to be proud of. So I built a Palace for the People when I laid out that state capitol building. Yeah, the common folks got a kick out of one of their own layin' around that fine new building . . . issuin' orders to men wearin' neck-ties . . . eatin' peach ice cream . . . and more'n likely, fartin' through silk.

We had somethin' goin', me and the people. Then that nutty young doctor forgot his Hippocratic Oath.

(The lights slowly go down to a twilight feeling.)

They say you can still see where the bullets creased the wall.

(A beat.)

I was on my way to a meeting – walkin' fast like I always did – and surrounded by so many bodyguards you'd have thought we might be goin' off to rob a bank. A young fellow stepped up past all those bodyguards like he wanted to shake hands. And I automatically reached out to oblige him. And the son-of-a-bitch *shot* me! With a gun he'd concealed in a handkerchief.

11

*(He gestures to a spot on his right side,
at the base of the rib cage.)*

Shot me right about . . . here. Hurt, too. Hurt like the very devil. Hell, I cut and run, my mama didn't raise no fool. *(A beat.)* Unless maybe it was my brother Earl.

My guards put sixty-one bullets in that goddamned assassin, by way of discouragin' his escape. That was pretty effective as far as it went . . . but it didn't save the Kingfish. I didn't last but a few hours after they got me to the hospital. *(A beat.)* I was forty-two years old. *(A beat.)* Last thing I said was "Who will take care of the people?" *(A longer beat.)* It's still a good question.

Lotta rumors went around after my death. Some folks said my bodyguards had been bought off, so they killed me and then shot a bystander they planted a gun on.

Some folks believed Standard Oil had me killed. I got no evidence they did. But I'm proud to say the big oil boys damn sure had *reasons* enough to kill me.

Others are convinced that Franklin D. Roosevelt had me shot, him bein' afraid I was replacin' him in the people's affection and scared I was gonna take that big tall chair away from him.

And I would have. All I needed was time.

(He jabs a forefinger at the audience.)

Listen, the Kingfish pulled Louisiana outta the mud! And

I'd a done the same thing for America, if I hadn't been cut short. Some folks didn't like my tactics, but you gotta fight fire with fire. I mean, you can *piss* on a fire and all you get is a funny smell. I had to make my enemies feel the heat.

(He takes a handkerchief from his pocket, swabs his neck and dry pats his forehead.)

When I took over, the Louisiana public roads were so bad the *weather* couldn't even get across the state! When I finished, Louisiana had the best damn roads in the nation. You can still see the bridges in Louisiana my administration built. One hundred and fifty-six of 'em. And neither time . . . nor weather . . . nor sandpaper . . . nor harsh words . . . has managed to erase my name, that somehow got carved on all of 'em in deep rock.

(He laughs.)

And hospitals? Why, when I took over I found hospitals and insane asylums right out of the London that ol' Charles Dickens wrote about. Saw scenes right outta the Dark Ages, yessir! People in chains and straitjackets! Bound up like so many bundles of wet wash, mewlin' and gurglin' in their own poor filth. And nobody to hear their screams or gibberish, whether prayerful or profane.

Well, the Kingfish changed all that. And he ain't come here to apologize for it.

The money-bag boys – and the Noo Awlins newspapers – whined that I spent more tax money in four years than the

13

four Louisiana governors before me had spent in *twelve* years. Goddamn right I did! But look what all I built! Them others, hell, they didn't build the people so much as a birdbath. The only time they knocked two boards together was to build new carts to haul off the public money they'd pilfered.

They accused me of raisin' taxes. And I stand guilty as charged. When you want ham, by God, you go to the smokehouse. The Kingfish went in that smokehouse and reached up high on the hog –

(He pantomimes it.)

– and cut off a few good slices of the very sweetest meat. And then he tossed it out to the poor ol' hungry yard dogs. And it was the first time in Louisiana's history they'd been tossed more'n table scraps or a dry bone.

(He wipes his palms on the handkerchief and returns it to his pocket.)

My only regret about taxes is I didn't live to collect more of 'em. A sensible tax structure is democracy's best tool. The one great *leveler* that can prevent the rise of a privileged class to lord it over everybody else and exploit 'em. *(A beat.)* That's the theory, anyhow. *(A beat.)* I wish Congress and our presidents would allow it to be tested.

My enemies did such a good job of *smearin'* me about taxes that to this day a lotta people think Huey Long put a tax on everything but secondhand doorknobs. But the truth is – and the record shows it – taxes went up by only

14

a little over two percent when I was runnin' things in Louisiana, as compared to the national average of nearly *five* percent. Why, the Kingfish did more with what he had to work with than anybody since . . . well, maybe since Jesus stretched out the loaves and fishes! And I'm bein' as modest about all this as circumstances permit.

(He chuckles.)

It was Winston Churchill – wadn't it? – that said, "He that tooteth not his own horn, the same shall not be tootethed!"

*(He grins and walks away from the small area
where he's paced and talked in the spotlight,
crosses to the cabin facade at deep stage left,
and sits in the rocking chair on the porch.)*

I grew up in the poor red hills of North Louisiana. The town of Winnfield, in Winn Parish. Little ol' town wadn't much bigger than a watch-fob. People joked it wadn't big enough to have a full-time village idiot, so we all had to take turns. The land around Winnfield wadn't fit for nothin' but raisin' billy goats and beans. Why, the Longs were so poor we didn't even have a chickenhouse! Our chickens had to roost on the edge of the *well*. Yessir, on the *well. (A beat.)* We sold a lotta eggs, but we never had anybody ask us for water.

(He laughs.)

But it's not any laughin' matter, bein' raggedy poor. Poverty's no more romantic than war. And either one can kill you.

A rich man's baby is gonna live where a poor man's baby is likely to die. Health records prove that all over the world, and I didn't tamper with the figures. Comin' into this world poor is like bein' dealt deuces and treys and then bein' told you gotta bet 'em against aces and kings.

Well, I didn't care for such odds. So I started out early to improve my cards. It wadn't easy. Took a lot of little mean, hardscrabble jobs and found no more joy in 'em than there is in bein' circumcised. Hard work's damn near as overrated as monogamy.

But one day, I found what I was good at. *(A beat.)* Sellin' things. Persuadin' folks.

> *(He stands, reaches behind the steps,*
> *and produces a tin bucket labeled "Cottolene";*
> *he holds the bucket up and pats it.)*

Sold Cottolene. C-O-T-T-O-L-E-N-E. It was a lard substitute derived from cottonseed oil, and the people that made it claimed it was purer and healthier than lard – and maybe it was. But that didn't change the fact I was tryin' to sell something that claimed to improve on the original.

> *(He turns, walks up to the porch of the cabin facade,*
> *takes off his hat, and bobs a bow to an invisible*
> *rural housewife.)*

Good afternoon, Ma'am, I'm Huey P. Long. From over here in Winn Parish? Yes, and I've come to talk to you about your family's good health. *(A beat.)* No Ma'am, I'm not a government man, just a friend and neighbor.

Now, I imagine you folks eat a lot of fried foods, don't you? *(A beat.)* Yes Ma'am, I like 'em myself, sure do. And I imagine you use lard to fry and bake, don't you? Plain ol' hog lard? Probably render it down yourself, I'd guess, in a big ol' backyard washpot just like my mama did.

(A beat.)

Uh-huh. Well, ya see, the problem with lard is . . . well, it just ain't *healthy*. And I didn't know that myself for years and years. But lard will turn to pure *fat* in your body. Clog up your bloodstream and pack around your heart till it can't breathe. Why, you'd just as well smother your heart with a goosedown pillow! Oh, yes Ma'am, I suspect there's more medical evidence against lard than there is against cancer and tuberculosis put together!

I suppose, now, that's why the Good Lord Himself warned folks against eatin' lard.

(A beat; shocked.)

You didn't *know* that? Oh, yessum, it's right there in the Bible! Surely you remember that part where the Lord warned the Children of Israel, "Eat not anything of the flesh of swine"?

Well now, *you* know – and *I* know – it just wouldn't be *like* the good, lovin' Lord to put the badmouth on anything as good as ham hocks and bacon and sow's head cheese, so it just stands to *reason* He was talkin' about lard! I know a lotta preachers that puts that exact interpretation on that particular passage of scripture. And I expect more preachers' wives cook with Cottolene than any other group – unless it's doctors' wives.

(A beat.)

Yessum, I know money's in real short supply. Most folks in these parts haven't seen anything green they could put in their pockets since they were kids goin' frog-giggin'. But I tell you what: you buy this bucket of Cottolene for cash money and I'll get two *more* buckets out of my car that I'll trade you for barter.

(A beat.)

Yessum, I'll be happy to take chickens and sweet potatoes in trade. Take nearly anything in the *world* but that terrible ol' hog lard.

(He comes down off the porch, grinning, and crosses to the apron at center stage.)

That Cottolene company started sponsoring baking contests to push their product. Offering prizes and what not. At one such contest, over in Shreveport, I walked up to a lovely black-haired honey-eyed girl named Rose McConnell. She'd just been declared the first-prize winner in cake baking.

(He takes off his hat and sweeps a grand bow.)

Good evenin' to ya, Miss McConnell. That's a mighty fine cake that has your name on it. But by your leave, Ma'am,

I'd like to ask you a personal question: Did you bake that cake yourself, or did your mama bake it?

(He jumps back in mock alarm.)

Why, here now, Miss Rose! No call to flash all that thunder-and-lightnin' outta those pretty dark eyes! It just seems to me you might be too *young* to be able to cook all that good.

(A beat.)

Say you really and truly baked it? Well now, not that I doubt your word . . . but I wish there was some way it could be *proved* to my satisfaction. Come to think on it, maybe there *is* a way . . .

(A beat.)

How? Why, invite me home to supper! I'd be honored to meet the family that produced a young lady as nice and graceful and lovely as you.

(A beat.)

Thursday? Yes, Miss Rose, I do believe I'm free on Thursday. You just name the hour and the street.

*(He turns to face the theater audience
and comes downstage.)*

Two and a half years later I married that girl. And later on I learned from Rose's sisters, by God, that her mama *had* baked that cake! *(Chuckles.)* That's when I knew Rose was gonna make the *perfect* political wife.

Sellin' Cottolene was all right for a young man. But I was gettin' old. *(Grins.)* Twenty-one. So I boned up readin' lawbooks and with the help of my brother Julius I got myself enrolled in the law school at Tulane University. And I finished law school in six months. Believe that? Yessir. Finished in *six months*.

(A beat.)

Now the big shots at Tulane will tell you right quick I didn't graduate. But I *finished*. And I learned enough law to pass the bar exam.

I was offered a partnership in Baton Rouge by two young lawyers in a firm called Peters and Strong. But I got to thinkin' about how it might sound to the public: Peters . . . Strong and Long.

And, besides, I wanted to run my own shop. You go in partners with somebody and it won't be long until each partner is convinced he does all the work and just gets half the money.

I went back to my hometown, hung out my shingle, took off my coat and started suing the banks and the big timber companies. My little brother Earl said, "Huey, ain't you afraid to take on all that money and power?" I said, "Earl, think about it: if they didn't have power and money they wouldn't be *fit* to sue!"

Those big timber companies were slashing across Louisiana like Jack the Ripper. Raping the land, cutting down everything in sight and not reseeding so much as one old stump. They bought the timber rights for a song, then ruined the land, and laughed in their counting houses. But I caught one of 'em swindlin' a poor old widow-woman. Well, you give the Kingfish good dough like that and he'll bake a batch of biscuits every time!

I'm tellin' ya, I stirred up a bigger stink than a sewer cleaner! And I made enough money out of whippin' the timber interests to finance my first venture into politics. I was all of twenty-four years old when I ran for state utilities commissioner, and the pundits gave me no more chance to win than a redbug swimmin' in kerosene.

But I had the hunger. I had the dream. I hit the campaign trail screaming bloody murder and demanding "the rascals" be tossed out. I campaigned nearly around the clock and invented the first sound truck so people could hear me hollerin' for miles before they could see me. And when they counted the votes, I was the new state utilities commissioner.

(A beat; he grins.)

And now the fox was in the henhouse!

First thing I did was force the big utility companies to give refunds to the people for all the years they'd been overcharging 'em. And just so there wouldn't be any doubt who ol' Santa Claus was, those rebate checks went out in envelopes with "Huey P. Long" printed on 'em in letters large enough to astonish the blind!

(He laughs; takes out his pocket handkerchief and swabs his neck again.)

Fighting the utility companies was a good warm-up for taking on Standard Oil. Every politician needs an enemy to whip up on and to hold up as a horrible example. And I'm here to tell ya that big corporations are the finest political enemies in the world. I imagine that's why God made 'em.

In time, I was ready to be governor. *(A beat.)* A political race, ya know, is really a small revolution – especially when you're attacking from *outside* the fort. And to get people in the mood for revolution, the first thing you've gotta do is get 'em all stirred up.

(He turns and walks toward center stage, rear, as a spotlight comes up on the podium there. The sound of cheering comes up, VOICE OVER, as HUEY addresses the podium, then it fades.)

So tonight, Governor Parker, I speak to you on behalf of the *plain* people of Louisiana . . . the people you have so long ignored and for whom you have shown the contempt of a mad king. Every citizen, Governor Parker, has the right to travel the road free – without dodging footpads, toll booths, or other bandits. So what's this pay-as-you-go policy you're yelpin' about? Sounds to me like you're talkin' about pay toilets! You go ahead and build your toll bridges, Governor – and Huey P. Long will build *free*

bridges right beside 'em. And *your* bridges will become
the most expensive buzzard roost in the world!

(Cheering, VOICE OVER, *up and out.)*

Now, my friends, let us consider the habits of animals.
A yearling, when he's twelve to fifteen months old, he
gets ashamed of living off somebody else and weans himself. And you take the pig – yes, even a ol' hog – *he* gets
ashamed of himself by the time he's shoat-sized and he'll
wean just like a yearling will. But you take a pie-eatin'
trough-feeder like my opponent, who's been suckin' the
pap for thirty-five years, and you can't wean him at all!
He'll still be tryin' to jump up in the trough when he's so
old he can't get his hind legs up!

(Cheering, VOICE OVER, *up and out.)*

I heard a story about the Governor over in LaFayette the
other day. It also involved a Chinaman, a Fiji Islander, and
a polecat. It seems the Chinaman, the Fiji fuzzy-wuzzy
and my opponent all made a bet who could stay in a closed
room the longest with the polecat. The Chinaman lasted
ten minutes and had to come out. The fuzzy-wuzzy lasted
twelve minutes, then *he* staggered out. Then it was my
opponent's turn. Wellsir, he no more than walked into the
room than the *polecat* ran out . . .

(Cheering, VOICE OVER, *up and out.)*

And it is here, in Arcadia Parish, under this oak, that
legend tells us Evangeline waited so long for her lover,
Gabriel, who never came. This oak is an immortal spot,

made so by Longfellow's poem. But Evangeline is not the only one who has waited here in disappointment.

Where are the schools that you have waited for your children to have – that have never come?

Where are the roads and highways that you send your money to build – that are no nearer now than ever before?

Where are the institutions to care for the sick and the disabled – that have never come?

Evangeline wept bitter tears in her disappointment . . . but they lasted only one lifetime. *Your* tears – in this country, around this oak – have lasted for generations. Give me the chance to dry the eyes of those who weep here!

(Cheering, VOICE OVER, *goes on and on as the spotlight dims and* THE KINGFISH *freezes in the pose with which he has ended the Evangeline Tree speech. When the spotlight goes dark, he walks from the podium toward the stage apron; lights come up there.)*

I know of only one truly fine political speaker who's come along since me.

Jack Kennedy.

And look what happened to both of us.

I wonder if they're trying to tell us something?

(He perches on the small stool at downstage center,
near the apron, in a spotlight.)

North Louisiana Protestants hate and fear the Catholics of South Louisiana – and vice versa. I wish the world wasn't made that way, but it is.

When I first went into South Louisiana, the only two Catholic words I knew were . . . "bingo" and "rhythm." *(He grins.)* But I learned fast.

(He stands atop the stool, as if addressing
a political rally.)

Yes, my friends, I love the Catholics and I love the Protestants. And it's not just because *God* loves both of 'em and would have me love 'em, too. No, it has to do with the way I was raised.

I can remember when I was a boy I'd get up early on Sunday morning and I'd harness up my old mule so I could go with my Catholic grandparents to early mass.

Then when I got back, I'd go to my *other* grandparents' home and I'd harness up the old mule so we could all go to the *Baptist* church.

And I'm here to tell you, my Catholic friends – as I tell my Protestant friends – my soul was made cleaner in *both* instances.

(He dismounts the stool.)

After I gave that speech down in South Louisiana one time, and we were on our way to the next town, one of my campaign workers said to me, "Mr. Long, I didn't know you had Catholic grandparents!"

(He looks up at the invisible campaign worker for a few beats.)

Hell, son, I didn't even have a *mule*!

(He laughs heartily and walks to the stage apron.)

When I first started out in politics, nobody wanted to give me money. People who bankroll politicians ain't interested in bettin' a dead horse. The more success and power I got, of course, the more the money rolled in. Political money men put me in the mind of a bunch of damn bankers – they only want to let you have money when you can prove you don't need it.

I remember fixing a bunch of bankers one time.

(He crosses to the desk at stage right, as it comes up in lights, and sits in the executive chair behind it, talking as he goes.)

I hadn't been governor long when my secretary told me a young lobbyist for the Banker's Association was standing on his head to see me. So I told her to send the bugger in.

(He rises to shake an imaginary hand.)

Come in, come in. Why, yes, I remember you; sure do. Have a seat. Now what can I do for you?

(He sits, cocks his head, and appears to listen.)

Uh-huh. Uh-huh. Yes. Right.

Now, everything you say is true; no doubt about it. I *did* tell you I thought the Banker's Association had a good bill and I *did* promise not to veto it. And I do recall the $10,000 contribution you folks made to my campaign, yessir.

Well, yes, it *is* true I vetoed your bill – but it don't mean I didn't appreciate your money. Ya see, a man just can't always read the future as clear as he'd like. You can understand that, can't you? There comes a time when a poor public man gets pulled from all directions and finds himself between a rock and a hard place.

You don't know what to tell your people? Well hell, son, that's simple.

(A beat.)

You just go tell 'em I lied.

(He stands.)

That's right, yes sir; you heard me right: you just go tell 'em I *lied*. A man can't ever go wrong telling the truth, and I hope you'll remember that. Glad I could help you out . . .

(He sits again, chuckling.)

The need of money in politics is constant and without end. When people are running against you, telling lies on you – or the truth when it hurts – a man's got to have money to fight back. And sometimes you have to be a little direct to make the lobbyists understand there won't be any milk if they let the cow go dry.

(He swings sideways in his chair to address an imaginary group of lobbyists, poking a forefinger at them.)

You fellows are all men of the world. And you know I'm gonna need money for that race that's comin' up. A *lotta* money.

(A beat.)

Well, now! I see that's makin' a few of you squirm and pull at your underwear. But I ain't seen a solitary twitch toward a billfold. Let me put it to you this way:

Those who give *now* will get the best cut of the pie.

Those who wait until just before the election to give will get what's left over.

And those who wait until *after* the election . . . will get "Good Gov'mint."

(He rises, walks around the desk, and perches on a corner of it.)

My enemies called me a thief and a grafter. But I never stole any money . . . to speak of. Nearly every nickel I laid my hands on went to fight my battles, and those battles were the *people's* battles. And it was their money to start with.

"Tom Sawyer in a toga," some people called me. Mebbe so. But I was the first southerner to have any original thoughts on government since Thomas Jefferson.

"A rustic Caesar," they called me. Said I abused power.

(A beat.)

I admit I never let power go to waste. Power's what makes the mule plow and the steamboat whistle. If I bent the rules a little, it was to get a better grip on the reins or the throttle. If I'd waited for "the slow and deliberate processes of government" to work – as the civics teachers wanted me to – why, hell, it would have given my opponents time enough to dynamite my plans. You've got to remember my enemies had the sociological instincts of the early primates, and enough money to burn a wet mule.

I was up against people that wanted to keep the whole pie for a privileged handful, and I was trying to *cut* the pie. So I slashed and whittled a little, yeah.

In one session I passed forty bills through the Louisiana legislature in five days. Yessir. Bills that changed the old ways of doing things, the basic rules. Some people complained I didn't print any copies of the bills. Said they'd been passed without anybody but me getting to read 'em. I said, "Hell, why not? Ain't anybody but me gonna *sign* 'em!"

(He rises, goes around the desk, and sits in the chair.)

The federal election officials got after me a time or two.

(He appears to be listening to visitors in his office.)

So your complaint, gentlemen, is that my opponent got only nine votes in the whole of Saint Barnard Parish?

Well, what's wrong with that? That's about the same number my opponent always gets in that parish.

Yes, gentlemen, I can explain how I got more votes in that parish than the total population is.

Ya see, the problem is one of bureaucratic inefficiency. That's right, "bureaucratic inefficiency." We gotta lot of people who live on houseboats along the bayous and back in the swamps. And your pussy-footin' federal census takers can't find 'em to count, because they're afraid of snakes and alligators and gettin' their feet wet. You federals are just gonna have to do a better job of countin' if you want *your* figures to tally with *my* votes. Nice to talk to you . . .

(He picks up the telephone, dials a number, and waits for it to ring; then he speaks into the phone.)

Hello, is this the head of the Barnum Bailey Circus performing here in Baton Rouge?

Well, good! This is Governor Huey Long. The Kingfish, right!

I got a little problem I think you can help me with. Ya see, tonight's our big Homecoming football game at Louisiana State University – LSU. We're gonna have a big pre-game parade, and I'm gonna lead the marching band. And when the football game starts, I'm gonna be down there on the sideline helpin' the coach. So you can see it's kind of a big night for me.

Now why I called you, Mr. Barnum Bailey, is to ask you to cancel your circus performance tonight.

Yessir, I said "cancel." We've just built a big new football stadium, ya see, and I'm afraid we can't fill it up if we have to compete with your circus. And it'd look bad – wouldn't it? – to build a big stadium like that and not have it full for the first Homecoming game. So if you just could see your way clear to –

(A long beat.)

Can't do it, huh? Not even as a personal favor to the *governor*?

(A beat.)

Well, that's mighty disappointin' to hear. I'd hoped to be able to persuade you.

31

(A beat.)

Uh-huh. Uh-huh. Oh, but – Mr. Barnum Bailey? – there is a *second* reason I called and I almost forgot it. I wanted to be sure you're conversant with our "Dip Law" here in Louisiana.

(A beat.)

I say our "Dip Law." You know about that, don't you?

(A beat.)

You *don't?* Well, I guess it's a good thing I called! Our law says that all animals being brought into Louisiana must be dipped in a compound that'll keep 'em free of lice and ticks and other such disease-carrying parasites . . . Uh-huh . . . So I'm asking Colonel Brown, of my state police, to hustle on out to your tents so he can *personally* assure me that all your lions and tigers and elephants and go-rillas gets dipped before tonight's performance.

(A long beat; he grins hugely.)

Is that right? Well, now, that's mighty neighborly of you, Mr. Barnum Bailey, and I surely do 'preciate it. And say . . . since you're not doin' anything tonight, why don't you take in a good football game?

(He hangs up the phone, laughing, then stands and walks to center stage where he encounters invisible newsmen.)

Ah, the members of the Fourth Estate! It's always a plea-
sure to deal with your accusations.

(A beat.)

Me, despise the free and inquiring *Press*? Where'd you
get that idea? Why, only this mornin' I was remarkin'
that I consider my association with you fine ladies and
gentlemen of the press to constitute one of life's *minor*
ecstasies . . .

(He grins.)

And as for your *bosses* – I mean your editors and publishers – take away their exaggerations, sensationalisms,
outright lies, self-righteousness and stupidity and I got
nothin' against them either.

(He points to one reporter.)

You, there. The Noo Awlins *Times-Picayune* reporter.
I read your paper's editorial jumpin' on me for playin'
"dirty politics" just because I hadn't paved Farm Road 86,
up north of Alexandria. I'm mighty disappointed in that.
Wadn't any "dirty politics" to it.

(A beat.)

Well, yes, that road *does* run by State Representative
Johnny Fontenot's farm and Johnny *has* voted against
most of my bills. But I don't see how your paper can accuse
me of holdin' a grudge against Johnny and bein' vindic-

tive. Ya see, this whole thing's a matter of friendship. *(A beat.)* That's right, friendship. My philosophy is "Always be *fair* to your enemies . . . and always be *partial* to your friends." And I'm simply gonna pave all my *friends'* roads before I get around to Johnny's.

What's that? *(A beat.)* Sure, I'm gonna run a clean campaign this year. I always run a clean campaign.

(He listens, then appears astonished.)

Well, all I *said* about my opponent's family, during that swing through North Louisiana, was "He's got one sister who's a *thespian* and another one, I hear, that's lived in a *uninterrupted monogamous relationship* for more'n twenty years!"

(A beat.)

I always tell the truth and let the chips fall where they may!

(He walks a few paces to stage left and confers with his henchmen.)

Earl, Andy, Leander, you other boys. Come here. Get about a hundred and fifty thousand of those new campaign circulars printed up. Don't print 'em on both sides this time. Our country folks are practical people, but they prefer not to get printer's ink on their backsides.

Earl, I want you to watch your drinkin' when we get up there in North Louisiana. That's Holy Ghost territory,

Earl, and more'n half the people believe Jesus just turned the water into *grape juice.*

And get the sound trucks ready to roll south to Cajun country, ya hear? Get crackin'! We got a campaign to win!

(He walks to the stage apron at center stage, takes off his coat and places it on the stool there, loosens his tie, and rolls up his shirtsleeves a couple of turns; during this we hear the sound of cheering, VOICE OVER, *coming up slowly; when it fades out he speaks as if making a campaign talk.)*

Now you know, and I know, that a newspaper editor will just naturally step over the truth – even if it's sleepin' in the middle of the road – to embrace a lie that's tryin' to run away from him. That's what the Noo Awlins *Picayune* did again the other day, when it attacked my road buildin' program.

We got a coffee-ground formation here in South Louisiana. The land sinks and shifts and just ain't stable. So it costs three times as much to build a mile of road *here* as it does in West Texas, where the ground is packed so hard a cat couldn't scratch it. But still that Noo Awlins *Picayune* bunch says they can't understand why we need to put a bigger tax on the rich man's heavy automobiles and the big oil company trucks. Why hell, I got a *baby brother* that can understand that and he ain't got but a third-grade education! The truth is, the *Picayune* understands; they just don't want *you* to understand. And as long as I've got the breath and the life and the backbone, I'll stand up and tell those newspaper egg-suckers what their lies are! And they *know* I'll tell 'em – and tell you the truth about 'em – and that's why they're against me!

(*Cheers,* VOICE OVER; THE KINGFISH
*acknowledges them with waves and nods. The cheers
fade. He looks bemused, hitches his thumbs in
his red suspenders.*)

They tell me that Mr. Rich, who lives in the big white house on the hill, didn't come out for my speech tonight.

Well, no reason he should have. I ain't likely to say anything that'll give him comfort.

There's no reason for Mr. Rich to vote for me . . . or for me to expect him to. He *owns* everything as far as the eye can see, even if you use a telescope, and I'm here sayin' he oughta be forced to share his wealth. I'm here tryin' to help you folks who pick up after Mr. Rich and live off his leftovers.

(*He is heating up.*)

Yes, face it. That's what people like you get. *Leftovers.* The scrapings in the bottom of the pan. The hind tit. And if Mr. Rich has his way, that's all you're ever gonna get. Far as he's concerned you can go to hell . . . and if you make it to heaven he'd have you greetin' Saint Peter barefoot and wearin' a gunnysack.

Not everbody likes to hear me talk like that. Not everbody likes to hear the truth.

So if you got on silk socks, you and Mr. Rich go on and vote for my opponent . . .

If you got on cotton socks, go vote for me.

Or if your cotton socks has holes in 'em – or if you don't have any socks a-tall – you oughta try to sneak in the polling place and vote for me *twice!*

(Cheers, VOICE OVER; THE KINGFISH *waves to the crowd, grins, then whirls and walks briskly toward the desk at stage right; the spotlight comes up there. He sits, grabs a newspaper off his desk, reads for a moment, and then picks up the telephone.)*

Alice? Is the lieutenant governor still waitin' out there? All right, send him in.

(He leans back in his chair, looking stern, and he does not rise when the lieutenant governor supposedly enters.)

Jimmy . . . let me refresh your memory. When I picked you to run on my ticket, I told you I expected two things of you: to keep your fly buttoned and your mouth shut.

(He takes the newspaper from the desktop and holds it out as if reading a headline.)

Now I see here in the paper "Lt. Governor Jimmy Noe calls for Two-Party System."

(He tosses the paper aside.)

Jimmy, why in hell are you encouragin' the goddamned Republicans to proliferate in Louisiana?

(A long beat.)

Oh. You thought it would be "healthy" to have a two-party system.

(A beat.)

You a doctor?

(Another long beat; shouting.)

I said are you a goddamn doctor?

And the answer is "No, Jimmy Noe ain't no kind of doctor!" So don't go prescribin' any more cures for Louisiana's political health. Ya *got* that?

(He calms himself; leans back.)

In the first place, Jimmy, we've already *got* what amounts to a two-party system in Louisiana: the pro-Longs and the anti-Longs. And that ought to be enough of a division for any goddamn state.

(He stabs a forefinger at him.)

You just remember this, Jimmy Noe: if an assassin should shoot you *dead* while you're standin' here talkin' to me – shoot you right between the *eyes* – the newspaper headlines would say "ASSASSIN'S BULLET *MISSES* HUEY LONG!"

(The stage lights go dim; we hear, VOICE OVER, *the rising babble and noises of a crowd;* THE KINGFISH *stands up from his chair, walks around the desk, cocks his head to listen for a few moments.
Then he approaches the stage apron; all lights go dark except the spotlight on him.)*

Hear that crowd outside? They've come down to the state capitol for the impeachment proceedings.

Can you imagine that? Those pissant legislators tryin' to impeach the *Kingfish*, and them not knowin' sheepdip from wild honey?

I've put their feet to the fire – held 'em accountable to me, and to the people they fooled into electin' 'em – and they don't like it.

So they're gonna try to impeach me.

Their problem is that I don't aim to stand for it. I intend to survive. And I'm not gonna worry about whether *they* survive.

When you take a whack at the reigning king, ya know, you better be sure you've hit him a killin' blow. It's been that way through history . . . and that's one rule I ain't about to change.

"Uneasy lies the head that wears a crown," ol' Billy Shakespeare said . . .

(He grins.)

Well, we'll see.

Right now, though, I gotta go shake the dew off my lily – and I expect you might want to do the same.

When you come back, I'll tell you how they tried to impeach the Kingfish.

(A beat.)

And what they got for their pains.

Blackout
and
END OF ACT ONE

*"When I took over, the Louisiana public roads
were so bad the weather couldn't even get across
the state! When I finished, Louisiana had the best
damn roads in the nation."*
The original stage Kingfish, John Daniel Reaves,
at New Playwrights' Theatre in Washington, D.C.
in the summer of 1979.
(Photo courtesy of New Playwrights' Theatre)

"My little brother Earl said, 'Huey, ain't you afraid to take on all that money and power?' I said, 'Earl, think about it: if they didn't have power and money they wouldn't be fit to sue!',"
John Daniel Reaves at New Playwrights' Theatre,
Washington, D.C., 1979.
(Photo courtesy of New Playwrights' Theatre)

"Those who give now *will get the best cut of the pie.*
Those who wait until just before the election to give
will get what's left over. And those who wait until after
the election . . . will get 'Good Gov'mint.'"
Ken Parnell points Huey Long's finger at
Harrell Performing Arts Theatre, Memphis, Tennessee, 1990.
(Photo courtesy of Paul Lormand)

*"Why, the Longs were so poor we didn't even have
a chickenhouse! Our chickens had to roost on the edge
of the well. Yessir, on the well! We sold a lotta eggs, but we
never had anybody ask us for water."*
Ken Parnell in production of *The Kingfish* at Harrell
Performing Arts Theatre, Memphis, Tennessee, 1990.
(Photo courtesy of Paul Lormand)

"When you take a whack at the reigning king, ya know, you better be sure you've hit him a killin' blow. It's been that way through history . . . and that's one rule I ain't about to change."
Ken Parnell at Harrell Performing Arts Theatre,
Memphis, Tennessee, 1990.
(Photo courtesy of Paul Lormand)

"*Some people claimed [O. K. Allen] got his name from sayin'* *'okay' to everything I told him to do. . . . O.K. might not of* *been any Quiz Kid, but he was my kinda man. Why, I could of* *picked his pocket and told him I was just lookin' for a match.*"
Ev Lunning, Jr., at Live Oak Theatre, Austin, Texas in 1990.
He repeated his role as Huey Long in 1991.
(Photo by Katie Kolodzey)

"Listen, the Kingfish pulled Louisiana outta the mud! And I'd
a done the same thing for America, if I hadn't been cut short."
John McConnell at John Houseman Theatre, New York,
during the 1991 Off-Broadway run of *The Kingfish*.
(Photo by Martha Swope Associates/Carol Rosegg)

John McConnell onstage at John Houseman Theatre, New
York, during 1991 Off-Broadway run of *The Kingfish*.
(*Photo by T. L. Boston*)

"They accused me of raisin' taxes. And I stand guilty as charged. When you want ham, by God, you go to the smokehouse. The Kingfish went in that smokehouse and reached up high on the hog – "
John McConnell at John Houseman Theatre, New York, during the 1991 Off-Broadway run of *The Kingfish*. (Photo by Martha Swope Associates/Carol Rosegg)

ACT TWO

The stage again opens dark. As lights go up on Huey Long's office, we see THE KINGFISH *pacing around his desk, highly agitated, as he addresses unseen henchmen and legislative supporters.*

THE KINGFISH

I call the legislature down here for a short session to pass a li'l ol' five-cents-a-barrel oil tax, and what happens? Those popinjays in the House vote *impeachment* charges!

How could they pop this on us, and so catch us by surprise? Earl, you're supposed to keep your ear to the ground. A goddamn freight train could sneak up on me if I depended on you!

Speaker Fournet, you don't even know what's goin' on in your own House! Why, hell, even a madam runnin' a whorehouse knows to take care of business! How'd you lose control?

All you had to do was adjourn the House without a vote, but you let a free-for-all break out and even let the other side take over the chair! My God, if you'd kept your head all you had to do was bang your goddamn gavel and bellow "I declare this House adjourned." But instead you stood around mumblin' the Constitution to yourself and lost *control!*

And now Daniel R. Weller of Standard Oil and his so-called "Dynamite Squad" has rented a whole damn floor of the Heidelberg Hotel to ramrod this impeachment thing out of.

(A beat.)

Well, boys, there's one thing about dynamite: it can go off in your hand if you ain't careful, and it don't care who it blows up. This day, my friends, will go down in Louisiana history as "Bloody Monday" – not "Black Monday." *(With gesture.)* "Lay on, MacDuff, and damn'd be him that first cries 'Hold, enough!'"

(He grabs a sheet of paper from his desk, snaps it out in front of him at arm's length and, donning a pair of reading glasses, prepares to read from it.)

Well, let's look at their charges. See what we're faced with beatin'.

(He perches on the corner of his desk and looks over his glasses at his henchmen.)

Hell, Leander, I don't even know what to *wear* to a god-damned impeachment.

(Reading from the charge sheet.)

"Count One: Controlling the judiciary."

Hell, you can't do anything for the people if you don't run the *courts*. That's fundamental civics.

"Count Two: Requiring undated resignations of his appointees."

That ain't against the law, is it? *(A beat.)* It *is*? Well, it's a silly goddamn law! How you gonna get anything done if you can't squeeze the bureaucrats and hold 'em accountable? Earl, make a note: when this impeachment farce is over with we're gonna repeal that silly-assed law.

"Count Three: Intimidating teachers."

Teachers my ass! All I did was fire the LSU football coach because he wasn't winnin'. If it's a crime to fire a football coach, we'll have to hang half the school boards in this country.

"Count Four: Misusing state funds."

You know what they're talkin' about there? My building programs. Ya see, every tax dollar I spend is a dollar less for them to steal. So to those Greedy Guses that's "misusing state funds."

"Count Five: Using abusive language."

(Astonished.)

Well I'll be goddamned!

(Peers over his glasses.)

Billy Shakespeare addressed that in one of his plays: "You

43

taught me language; and my profit on't is, I know how to curse. The red plague rid you for learning me your language."

(A beat.)

Huh? (A beat.) Earl, I didn't *expect* you to understand it. Don't worry about it.

"Count Six: Engaging in immoral behavior in a Noo Awlins night club."

(He flicks a quick look at the audience
and rapidly turns the page.)

"Count Seven: Attempting to intimidate the press."

Ah, just because I warned that Baton Rouge publisher I was gonna tell everbody about his brother being in the nuthouse. Hell, the names of folks in the state nuthouse is public information; I can tell any-goddamn-body I want to. Whatever happened to freedom of speech?

"Count Eight: Endeavoring to hire one Battling Bozeman to kill J. Y. Sanders."

The truth is, I *fired* Bozeman as my bodyguard because he's so crazy I'd rather take my chances with an assassin. It made Bozeman as hot as a staked-out dog, so he started makin' up wild stories for the opposition.

(He looks over the rims of his reading glasses.)

Now, I'll *admit* that anybody that killed J. Y. Sanders would be doin' the world a fifty-dollar favor – but I didn't suggest it to Bozeman or anybody else.

"Count Nine: Using the militia to pillage private property."

Hah! The "private property" was illegal and cheatin' gamblin' joints I closed all over this state. Hell, I *had* to call out the militia! I couldn't depend on the crooked local law enforcement officers in some of those parishes. Why, some of 'em wouldn't finger a prostitute.

(Laughs.)

"Count Ten: Usurping the powers of the legislature."

(He repeats the charge, spacing the words.)

Now we're gettin' down to the licklog, to the *crux* of the matter. What I'm *really* guilty of is interposin' myself between the legislators and their special-interest bosses. If they want that charge to be accurate, they ought to amend it to "Throwing thieves out of work."

(He tosses the charge sheet on his desk.)

Boys, we gotta seize the initiative. The lyin' press is tryin' to convict and hang me without a trial. Freedom of the press bein' limited to those who *own* one, I'm gonna start my own newspaper. We'll call it . . . uh . . . *The Louisiana Progress*. And we'll finance it outta the Deduct Box and print the news like *we* want to. And why not? That's what other publishers do.

(A beat.)

Well yes, Mr. Speaker, I expect my enemies will scream about it. They've been screamin' about the Deduct Box since I first set it up. But what's wrong with havin' our state employees voluntarily contribute 10% of their salaries to the Deduct Box? They wouldn't *have* their jobs if it wasn't for me, and if I get beat they'll lose 'em! I reckon that's why 100% of our fine state employees have "volunteered" to have the deduct taken directly out of their paychecks, don't you?

(He grabs another sheet of paper off his desk and thrusts it out at someone.)

Leander, I want you to start preparin' my defense before the senate. Here's the lawyers I wanta use.

(A beat.)

Which one? Hell, all eight of 'em! Didn't you ever hear of insurance?

Earl, call Rose over in Shreveport and tell her to come on down here to stand by my side. And tell her to bring a white dress. I want everbody around me lookin' as saintly as possible.

(He grins.)

'Course now, Earl, that may mean *you* will have to stay out of sight for awhile.

(To the group.)

All right, all you boys shuck on outta here and build some fires under people. I got phone calls to make.

(He sits at the desk, dials a number, and speaks into the telephone.)

Senator Snell? It's the Kingfish. I sure am sorry to know you're bad sick.

You're *not* sick? Why, Senator, that absolutely astonishes me! When you didn't show up with the other boys today, I figured you to be paralyzed from the Adam's apple down. Much as I've done for you, I thought you'd crawl naked over broke glass to rally 'round my flag.

Uh-huh. I see. Well, Senator, I'm not an unreasonable man. Puttin' it as delicately as it deserves . . . what's your goddamn price?

(He listens, nodding.)

I count five new patronage jobs, a highway, a bridge, and an improved committee assignment for yourself.

(A beat.)

How you fixed for toilet paper and razor blades?

(A beat.)

Senator, the only difference between you and a hog is that a hog jerks when he pisses! *(A beat.)* Hold on, Senator! I didn't say "No." *Of course* you'll get what you want. All you've got to do is sign a paper – we're callin' it "The Round Robin" – that says (a) you won't support any impeachment charges now pending against me and (b) you won't support any *new* charges those bastard Dynamite Squadders might think up. That's reasonable, ain't it?

(A beat.)

Well, Senator, if I have to go to actual *trial* I'm prepared to offer a three-pronged defense: One, I didn't do it. Two, if I *did* do it, I didn't *go* to do it. And three, if they'll let me go, I won't do it any more.

(He laughs.)

But if enough of you boys sign that Round Robin, there won't be any goddamn trial. The other side'll just be pissin' in the wind.

(Cheerfully.)

Senator, I'm mighty proud to know you've got the ability to rise above mere principle. I'll send Earl right over with that Round Robin paper.

(He hangs up the telephone.)

And that'll be the last thing you'll get from me, you black-mailin' son-of-a-bitch!

(Blackout. Then we hear, VOICE OVER, *sounds of shouting and catcalls. Voices call "Point of Order, Mr. President"* . . . *"This is an outrage"* . . . *and so on. When lights come up,* THE KINGFISH *is at center stage and speaking to his wife.)*

Listen to that commotion, Rose! Is anything sweeter than knowing your enemies are having conniptions and nothing will come of it? As ol' Billy Shakespeare wrote, it's all "sound and fury, signifying nothing . . ."

Ah, Rose, Rose, I had a *majority* on that Round Robin paper. They can howl till doomsday without being able to change a thing!

I propose a toast.

(He mimes a toasting gesture.)

To the first lady of Louisiana, the lovely Rose McConnell Long! And long may she reign!

(He mimes drinking.)

And, if it's not too immodest, I propose a second toast.

(Again, miming a toasting gesture.)

To His Excellency, the Honorable Huey Pierce Long –

still governor of the great state of Louisiana, by the grace of God and the people . . . and with a little help from the moderately greedy.

(He laughs and again mimes drinking.)

Rose, I swear, I hadda make more promises these last few days than a boy wrestlin' in a rumble seat – to get those Round Robin signatures. But it worked, Rose! We turned im*peach*ment into peaches and cream!

(A beat.)

Now I got to *keep* all those promises.

(A long beat.)

Most of 'em.

Aw, I can worry about that another day. Right now the governor would like to dance with the first lady!

(We hear, VOICE OVER, the strains of a waltz; THE KINGFISH dances with his lady as the lights go dim to blackout. At lights up, he walks downstage, taking another cigar from his pocket, unwrapping it, and speaking to the audience from the stage apron.)

Not long after that I started seriously thinkin' of takin' on the *national* champion.

(He inserts the cigar in his mouth, lifts his head, and juts his jaw in imitation of FDR and his famous

cigarette holder. Looking down his nose in the imperious
FDR manner, he speaks through clenched teeth.)

Mistah Franklin Del-no Roosevelt!

(He removes the cigar, grins.)

Originally I was stronger for FDR than horseradish. And
Roosevelt did some good things, sure. But he wasn't a
bump on a pickle compared to what I would have been in
the White House.

(A beat.)

FDR had some good ideas and some good instincts. But
he didn't act on them as boldly as he should have. That
silver spoon kept gaggin' him. Groton and Harvard and
good manners and worryin' about being a "gentleman"
made him cautious. *(A beat.)* I wasn't handicapped by any
such baggage. Where FDR used the scalpel, I was more
of a meat-ax man. I was in a hurry.

But before I could run for president, I had to win a seat
in the United States Senate – to use as a national forum.

Never was any doubt in my mind I could win a Senate
seat. My problem was my friends – and my brother Earl.
Everbody and his dog lined up to run for governor when
they saw I was about to run for the Senate. I couldn't
have that . . .

*(He turns and walks back to his desk, which comes up in
the spotlight, and takes a seat in the executive chair.)*

No, Earl, I can't let you be governor. Not yet, anyhow.

(A beat.)

I *know* you're my brother, Earl. That's the main thing you got goin' against you. I'm tryin' to avoid the accusation that we're settin' up a Long dynasty down here. Louisianians don't take to royalty, Earl. They wouldn't like the governor's chair handed down by right-of-birth. *(A beat.)* And to tell the truth, Earl, I don't want folks to get confused as to which Long is runnin' the show.

I've already made up my mind that O. K. Allen is gonna succeed me as governor. Ya see, Earl, when I quit this chair I want a man in it who'll be satisfied with the purely ceremonial . . . a man who'll be grateful to me every time he picks up his paycheck. Yes, a figurehead. And if *you* get to be governor, Earl, I wouldn't any more'n turn my back than you'd start a war with Oklahoma or Arkansas. You'd wanta be in *charge*, Earl, I know ya!

(A beat.)

Well, suit yourself. But I'm tellin' ya – if you run, you're strictly on your own. Just remember that in Louisiana you got to be *fer* the Kingfish or *agin* the Kingfish. That's the rule, Little Brother, and you ain't gonna be no exception. Bide your time, Earl. You're young. Hell, once I get the White House you can be anydamnthing you wanta be – and that's a promise.

(Lights go down on the desk area; THE KINGFISH *walks from behind it and addresses the audience.)*

I won my race for the United States Senate from here to Timbuktu. Actually, my opponent didn't put up much of a fight. I even carried Noo Awlins big. Election night was sort of an anticlimax.

The only troublesome incident occurred when one of my cohorts got riled about a patronage job he didn't get and threatened to reveal some intimate secrets. We managed to get the gentleman out of his hotel before he could go through with the press conference he'd called, and take him on a long fishin' trip until the election was safely past.

'Course now, the damn fellow didn't seem to appreciate his fishin' trip as much as he might have, and told a different version about what had happened. The newspaper boys came to me about it.

(He turns to talk with newsmen.)

Kidnapped?

Gentlemen, in order for somebody to be kidnapped they have to be held for ransom, don't they? Can you think of anybody that'd be willin' to pay to get that sorry bastard back? I rest my case!

Detained?

Well now, it seems to me like you boys are quibblin' over semantics. Far as I know it was a fishin' trip, pure and simple. Maybe if the fish had been bitin' he'd see it that way too.

What am I gonna *do* about it? Well, I ain't gonna make the damn fellow a *game warden* – he don't appreciate outdoor sports!

(He walks down to the stage apron.)

Even though I'd been elected U.S. senator, I couldn't leave the state as long as Paul St. Cyr was lieutenant governor. St. Cyr, ya see, carried a burdensome load of ambition and I couldn't resign my seat because he'd step up and proclaim himself acting governor. He was trying to occupy the office so as to keep my handpicked man from taking over.

I even declined to take part in the dedication of a new bridge over the Mississippi River because the ceremonies would have involved my stepping across the state line for a few minutes. And as for going to Washington to take my Senate oath – well, that was out of the question. I just let the Senate start its new session without me and hunkered down in the governor's office.

St. Cyr thought he'd found a way to get rid of me. He had a notary public swear him in as governor on the grounds that I had been elected United States senator – and had, therefore, automatically abdicated as governor.

(He turns, goes back to his desk as the lights come up there, and speaks while crossing.)

Leander, where are we legally in this mess? Can a god-damn notary public swear a man in as governor and make it stick?

(He sits behind his desk.)

Maybe so, huh? It might be legal?

(He thinks for a few beats, then brightens.)

Well, good.

I say "Good." Now, here's what I want you to do. Beginning tomorrow – and every day this week – in every parish in Louisiana, I want ten or fifteen or twenty people to go before notary publics and get themselves sworn in as governor.

That's right, Leander. By Sunday I want the newspapers full of stories about *hundreds* of Louisiana citizens who've taken the oath as governor in that exact manner.

(He laughs.)

Why, we'll laugh that son-of-a-bitchin' St. Cyr out of the state, halfway across Texas, and into the sorriest precincts in Oklahoma!

*(He holds up his right hand as if taking an oath.
Big grin.)*

I swear!

(He laughs and turns away, then has an afterthought.)

And, oh, Leander? You just be sure *Earl* ain't one of 'em that takes that oath. *He* might make it stick!

(Lights go down on the desk area; THE KINGFISH *advances to center stage and addresses the audience.)*

My supreme court held all those instant "governors" – including Mr. Prissybritches St. Cyr – to be fraudulent claimants. Then we gave Paul St. Cyr a dose of his own medicine. My court held that when St. Cyr *unconstitutionally* took the oath as governor, he had abandoned his *own* office. *(A beat.)* The poor bastard had to go out and find honest work.

Me? Well, I got to appoint me a tame fella – a caretaker – and then I went off to Washington knowing I could sleep at night.

Soon after I got to Washington, a survey of tourists showed that when people came to visit their nation's capitol, they wanted to see three things: the White House . . . the Washington Monument . . . and the Kingfish.

I gotta admit I wasn't near that popular with my Senate colleagues. No, for I wouldn't play the game. The Senate was a place where people scratched each other's backs. The Senate called itself "the greatest deliberative body in the world" and put such a stock in formal courtesies that thieves, mountebanks, and liars could call each other "my distinguished and able colleague" and keep a straight face.

When Senator Joe Robinson of Arkansas denounced me for attacking his tax bill as favoring the rich – because I had read to the Senate a list of *forty-three* big corporations that'd signed up as Robinson's law clients, each of which would have benefitted from his tax bill – half the damn chamber attacked the poor ol' Kingfish. You'd have thought I'd turned a polecat loose in that "august body."

Senators Walter George of Georgia . . . Millard Tydings of Maryland . . . Reed of Pennsylvania, and a lot of others . . . said I was "utterly lacking in sensibilities." Said I had "no concept of courtesy." And so on and so forth and blah-blah-blah. One senator flat accused me of calling my colleagues "crooks." So I quickly said, "Gentlemen" –

(Here he speaks with elaborate mock courtesy and makes oratorical gestures bordering on parody.)

– "I want here and now to disclaim that I have the *slightest* motive for saying, or that in my heart I believe, that a United States senator could to the *slightest* degree be influenced in any vote which he casts in this body . . .

(A beat.)

. . . by the mere *fact* that association might mean hundreds of thousands or even millions of dollars in the way of lucrative fees."

I didn't care what my colleagues thought. If other senators wanted to banish me to a corner and leave me to talk to myself, at least I'd be talking to somebody with good sense. And wouldn't anybody be asking me for anything.

The nearer I got to being president, the more my enemies got after me and the worse the newspapers became in evaluating my character. They said Jesse James was a gentleman compared to me, and *he* had the decency to

57

wear a mask . . . They said I had the face of a clown . . . the heart of a burglar . . . and the disposition of a tyrant . . . that I was a "degenerate in mind and morals."

My enemies hated me for what I tried to accomplish. And I hated them for standing in my way. We didn't play patty-cake with each other.

(He turns and walks toward the podium as lights come up; campaign music is heard, VOICE OVER. *Standing in a spotlight at the podium,* THE KINGFISH *stills the music with an abrupt gesture.)*

My opponents say they want to get "Longism" out of Louisiana. That "Longism" must be destroyed. *(A beat.)* Know what that requires?

The first thing they'll have to do to erase "Longism" is blow up about five thousand miles of new roads and more than a hundred bridges.

Then they'll have to burn dozens of hospitals, and snatch free books from the hands of every little school child in Louisiana.

Then they'll have to lay off twenty-two thousand men gainfully employed in the construction of hundreds of useful public works projects.

Yessir, if they wanta erase "Longism" in Louisiana, that's what they've got to do just to make a *start*!

(Cheering, VOICE OVER, *up and out.)*

I'm proud of what "Longism" has done for Louisiana. *America* needs a dose of "Longism" if you're asking me.

Why, we've got more food in America than we could eat if we didn't plow a row or fatten a hog for the next three years – and yet Americans are starving!

We've got enough cotton, wool, and leather to last three years if we didn't raise another boll of cotton, shear another sheep, or tan another hide – and yet Americans are ragged and without clothes!

We have more houses than ever before – yet many are empty for want of mortgage money, while Americans are homeless and hopeless without shelter.

Why? Because a handful of rich men own *everything*. The masses own nothing. About a dozen men dominate the vast majority of wealth in this country. They couldn't spend all the money they've got if they started trying today and spent with both hands till they got to the cemetery . . . and them and their pet pigs couldn't eat one percent of the food if they stuffed their gullets for a lifetime.

In biblical times, you know, there was a freeing of debt every seven years and the wealth was redistributed every fifty years. If you don't believe that, you ain't read the Book of Leviticus. If it worked then, why can't we resurrect it?

My opponents say, "Oh, but you can't do that in modern times."

The *hell* you can't! We can start by putting a tax on large gifts and on big estates . . . so a class of economic royalists won't exist in perpetuity. Why should Mr. Rich's baby come into this world owning a hundred times – a *thousand* times – more money than your baby, born the same day, can accumulate if he lives to be ninety-nine years old and works hard every day of his life? We can redistribute the wealth through a graduated income tax, that will put money to good uses for the people instead of it wallowing around idle and multiplying itself for Mr. Rich and his sons and grandsons and great-grandsons.

We need to *share* the wealth! Let's put the jam jar on the lower shelf, where the *little man* can reach it!

There is no logical reason why – in this blessed land of plenty – every man should not own a five-thousand-dollar debt-free home . . . and a car . . . and a radio . . . and have an annual income of three thousand dollars.

"Pie in the sky," my opponents say. "Can't be done," they say. And I say to them, "Hide and *watch* me! I'll show you how to do it!

All it takes is one public man – yes, one politician – who ain't afraid of his shadow and won't lick the boots of Mr. Rich.

I'm organizin' Share-the-Wealth clubs all over the United States of America. I'm goin' on the radio tellin' the *plain* people to organize their Share-the-Wealth clubs in their hometowns and help me make Every Man a King.

I'll leave you tonight with the words of my campaign song, and I hope you'll think about what they mean:

> "Why weep or slumber, America?
> Land of the brave and true?
> With castles, clothing and food for all,
> *All* belongs to you."

(Cheering, VOICE OVER, *as* THE KINGFISH *leaves the podium and, wiping his neck with a handkerchief, walks down to center stage to address the audience.)*

It wasn't long until President Roosevelt got to fretting that I might give him more competition than he'd bargained for. Share-the-Wealth clubs were proliferatin' all over the country. Roosevelt decided he had to stop me. He started using hardball tactics. Tough tactics. Tactics that . . . sorta reminded me of myself.

(A beat.)

So I got an appointment to go see him in the White House.

(He puts on his hat and strolls down to the stage apron.)

Mr. President, how are ya?

(Leans down to mime shaking hands, then looks all around the "office.")

My, my! The Oval Room at Sixteen Hundred Pennsylvania Avenue. I don't guess the cotton gets any taller'n this, does it?

(He grins, and sits on the stool as if facing the president's desk.)

No, thank you, Mr. President; I'll just keep my hat on. I likely won't be here very long.

(Again inspecting the "office.")

This trip.

(Comes back to reality.)

Mr. President, as you know, I've supported you from scratch. Helped put you here among all this splendor and the artifacts of history. And I've supported your programs in the main. And what are my thanks? Why, you've taken all the federal patronage away from me in Louisiana and you're hirin' nobody but *anti*-Long people in federal jobs down there! The only way I can accurately describe such actions, Mr. President, is to say they're close kin to the feces of a species of the poultry variety.

(He holds up a hand to interrupt.)

I've *got* respect for your high office. It's *you* I'm havin' the trouble with!

(A beat.)

Well, yes, I *have* been critical of you lately. There are

breadlines and soup kitchens out there, Mr. President, in the richest nation God has ever blessed! You can abolish misery and poverty and bring hope – all by crackin' your whip.

(A beat.)

What do you mean "limitations." You're *president!* Who the hell outranks *you?*

(Snorts.)

Congress! Congress ain't nothin' but a disorganized mob! Smart as you are you oughta be able to flatter a third of 'em into doin' what you want, and *scare* or *bribe* another third into it . . . and the final third won't make any difference!

Look what I've done in Louisiana – and I'm just a little ol' mudbog governor! We're buildin' more in Louisiana than anywhere else, we got more people at work, and there's no end in sight! Now, my enemies say I'm a communist, but in truth I'm the pluperfect quintessential capitalist. Yessir! Because I want *everybody* to own property and share the wealth.

And I've been told, Mr. President, that you think General Douglas MacArthur and myself are the two most dangerous men in America! No, no, it's all right; no need to be embarrassed. *(A beat.)* I agree with you about the General myself.

But I'm not a dictator, Mr. President, or a communist. A

populist, maybe. I believe it's my job to see that people have a right to share in what they build.

Now, I can only conclude that you don't understand my mission. Because my people tell me you've sent 250 treasury agents to Louisiana to turn up income tax violations on me! *Me* – one of your earliest and most loyal supporters!

(Listens a bit; nods.)

Uh-huh. I see. Well, it don't surprise me my enemies *told* you that. What surprises me is you're *listenin'* to 'em. I can tell you right now you're wastin' time and money. Your agents can dig up the whole state of Louisiana and all they're gonna find is oil, grubworms, and the bones of my enemies!

(Listens.)

An "accommodation"?

(A beat.)

Well, Mr. President, can you define that "accommodation"?

(A beat.)

Oh, I think I know what you're drivin' at. I'd just like to hear you say it.

(He stands.)

Mr. President, I'm the Kingfish . . . not the Crawfish. Good day to you, suh!

(He turns and strides rapidly away to center stage; then comes halfway back to address the audience.)

I got a little hot under the collar on that occasion.

It was obvious to me the President's price for callin' off his investigative dogs was my silence and my "reconsiderin'" my presidential ambitions . . . even though he was too "refined" to say so outright. Sometimes "gentlemen" are handicapped in politics. It ain't really a gentlemanly callin' . . .

Still, Roosevelt *was* a good politician. In truth he was about the smoothest, slickest operator I ever ran up against. It was hard to get a hand-hold on him.

I think I caught FDR by surprise on that first visit. The next time I saw him, the President commenced talkin' the minute I got my foot in the door and didn't give me anymore chance to talk back than if I'd come down with lockjaw.

I never met a man that could do me that way before. *(A beat.)* One of my great regrets was that we didn't get to run against one another. It would have been a better show than the circus.

(A long beat; he muses, unwraps a cigar.)

I don't believe politicians go all out for their friends like they used to. With television, they think they don't need each other or even need their political parties. There's no bond, no union like we once had. Politicians nowadays remind me of wet cellophane tape: you can see right through 'em, and they won't stick to nothin' or nobody for long.

It used to be different. Hattie Caraway of Arkansas succeeded to her husband's Senate seat when he died. Everbody assumed she'd serve out his unexpired term and go back home . . . like they thought a proper lady should. But when Hattie decided to fight for the seat in her own right, I liked her spunk and went around to see her.

(He turns to talk to her.)

Hattie, they're sayin' you don't have a snowball's chance in the Devil's precincts. You've got six political heavyweights runnin' against you, you got no organization, no rich backers, and the hardest thing of all is, you're a woman.

But you're a good senator, Hattie. You've voted with me on the side of the common people. So I'm gonna invade Arkansas and tell your folks to send you back to the U.S. Senate. I'll bring my organization and I'll make ten speeches a day the last ten days of the campaign. Will that do?

(Grins.)

Fine, fine. I believe we can slip up on 'em, Hattie.

(He walks down near the stage apron and is picked up by a spotlight as he makes a campaign speech.)

I'm here in Arkansas to help pull a lot of fat-cat, pie-eatin' politicians off a little woman's back.

Hattie Caraway has courage and vision. She's fought the millionaires who have a stranglehold on this country. She didn't go to Washington and cozy up to the lobbyists and she didn't play footsie with other senators in their private club. She didn't go along to get along.

Senator Caraway voted for my proposal to limit personal income to a million dollars a year to any one individual. Now, you'd think *anybody* could get along on a million dollars a year, wouldn't ya? Well, lemme tell ya, a *majority* in the United States Senate couldn't *see* that! They worried that poor old Mr. Rich couldn't make it on one measly, lousy million dollars a year! Why, wouldn't that be terrible? It'd mean if Mr. Moneybags had to go to the toilet, he wouldn't be but about five hundred dollars richer by the time he got his pants up!

Hattie Caraway's doin' more for you people than FDR and his so-called "Brain Trust" and ever' New Deal bureaucrat in Washington. About all you're gettin' from them is *promises*. Promises are like cryin' babies – they ought to be carried out! You got promises from Franklin Roosevelt, but you're gettin' the same cackle, cluck, and strut that you got from Herbert Hoover.

I used to sell a patent medicine. Folks got their choice between *High* Popalorum or *Low* Popalorum. It came from the bark of the same tree, but to get the *High* Popalorum you skinned the tree from the bottom up . . .

(He mimes it.)

. . . and to get the *Low* Popalorum you skinned it from the top down.

(He mimes it.)

And it's just that way with Mr. Hoover and Mr. Roosevelt: it just depends on whether you want to be skinned from the ear *down* or the ankle *up*!

Send Hattie Caraway back to the Senate to help me fight for you! Do somethin' for the *little* man by votin' for a brave little woman!

(Cheering, VOICE OVER, *up and out;*
THE KINGFISH *turns aside and shakes hands with "Hattie.")*

It's a miracle, Hattie, you won! You're the first woman *ever* elected to a full term in the United States Senate. Why, Hattie, you'll be in the history books with me!

(He grins.)

Well, thanks, Hattie; I was glad to help. Just remember that you owe the Kingfish a big one . . .

(He walks down to the stage apron.)

I was just beginning to get my political ducks lined up in a row . . . when it happened.

(Stage lights go to dim; a twilight effect.)

It was a Sunday night . . . in September, 19-and-35. I'd come down from Washington and through O. K. Allen had called the Louisiana legislature into special session down in Baton Rouge . . . to pass a bill placing the hiring of all state teachers under my control . . . just to show FDR I didn't necessarily need to control *federal* jobs in Louisiana.

I also intended to shove through a bill to make it a crime in Louisiana for anybody – *anybody* – to infringe on states' rights. I figured that might slow down Franklin Roosevelt's march through Louisiana while my enemies cheered him, and put the power back where it belonged.

(A beat.)

I was coming from a meeting with some of my floor leaders.

(He turns to his assistants.)

Has everbody been notified of the early caucus tomorrow? Now, get a dozen of the boys to comb all the bars about ten o'clock, pull all of our votes out and start soberin' up the drunks. I need everbody as clear-headed as possible early in the mornin'. The other side's screamin' bloody murder that my bills violate the Louisiana Constitution. Hell, don't they know I *am* the Louisiana Constitution?

69

(He laughs briefly; then addresses the audience.)

I saw the chief justice of my court, Justice Fournet, over near the elevator. And as I started over to meet him a skinny young fella in a white suit came towards me, and I reached out to shake hands –

(Stage goes to black; loud gunfire is heard, VOICE OVER, *then a startled yell and scuffling sounds; then a series of shots: different guns, ricochet effects, a real burst of firepower. Then we hear the sound of an ambulance siren wailing. From the dark we hear* THE KINGFISH, VOICE OVER.)

Pray for me, Sister.

How's my blood pressure? That's bad. Isn't that bad?

(Heavy breathing.)

Who was it shot me? Dr. Who? Who the hell is he?

(Heavy breathing.)

I want Dr. Sanderson from Shreveport and Dr. Maes and Dr. Rives from Noo Awlins to do the operatin' on me. Nobody else.

(Heavy breathing. A spotlight falls on the hat THE KINGFISH *was wearing when he was shot, near center stage. That will be the only light used through the remainder of the play.)*

What do you mean my doctors can't get here in time? Who's gonna operate?

(Heavy breathing.)

My God, I appointed that doctor to the hospital board because he was starvin' to death in private practice! Sister, this is a bad time for a joke.

(Breathing becomes more labored.)

I need to talk to Earl . . . and Leander . . . and to Rose.

(Heavy breathing.)

She won the cake-bakin' contest . . . down in Shreveport.

(Breathing now more difficult.)

No! I can't talk to you about the Deduct Box now. *No*, I moved it. I'll tell ya later . . .

(Delirious, rambling.)

The roads are muddy . . . The farmers can't get out to vote . . . . We still got a lot to get done . . . . Look at that crowd, boys . . . Waving and smiling . . .

(Extremely labored breathing.)

There's . . . so much . . . to be done. . . . Who . . . will take care . . . of the people?

(Labored breathing. It abruptly ends. In the instant it does, the spotlight goes off and the stage is in blackout. We hear, faintly, the music of "Every Man a King"; it increases in volume, the lights slowly come up, and THE KINGFISH, *grinning and waving, bounds out to take his bows.)*

THE END

ABOUT THE AUTHORS

LARRY L. KING is co-author of the smash Broadway musical comedy *The Best Little Whorehouse in Texas*. His other plays are *The Night Hank Williams Died, Christmas: 1933*, and *The Golden Shadows Old West Museum*. He has won numerous honors for his journalistic and other writings and has been nominated for both a Tony Award and a National Book Award. BEN Z. GRANT, who grew up in Huey Long's Louisiana, has written short stories and has taught English, speech, and journalism. His play, *From Hardscrabble*, had its debut in 1990 at East Texas Baptist University.